One Body In Christ

ONE BODY IN CHRIST

by Kokichi Kurosaki

Edited and Revised by John Myers

VOICE CHRISTIAN PUBLICATIONS, INC.

BOX 672   NORTHRIDGE, CALIFORNIA 91326

© 1968
Voice Christian Publications, Inc.

First Printing
March, 1968

Second Printing
June, 1968

Contents

Introduction

Christians today are reaching out in many different directions in a sincere effort to meet the awesome challenge of the closing days of this dispensation. Everywhere we see evidence that the "mystery of iniquity" is coming to its head, in fearsome defiance of all that Christianity stands for. However, some inner spiritual sense tells us that God has an answer for this mighty *Goliath,* and we are reaching for that answer.

I personally believe that most of this reaching is good and that each emphasis is part of the greater answer we seek. However, at the very heart of things there is a deep-seated problem which if not met will finally disannul all other victories we may achieve. Scripture tells us this — and, thus far, the glorious but sad history of the Church bears ample witness.

It is with this root need that our Japanese brother so ably addresses himself in these pages — not merely pointing out the problem, but with rare spiritual insight giving the answer. I deem his work to be one of the outstanding books of our day and the spiritual concept he sets forth as absolutely essential to the realization of New Testament "fullness".

John Myers, *President*
Voice Christian Publications

CHAPTER ONE

Our Present Dilemma

E UROPEANS AND AMERICANS, having been under the divided conditions of the existing system of Christian churches for many centuries, find it almost impossible to grasp an idea quite different from what they have known. Especially is this true since the European civilization is dominated by the influence of the Greek and Roman civilizations. Western Christianity could not help being also strongly influenced by these cultures.

Under Roman influence Christianity became very institutional, while Greek culture produced strong theological and philosophical tendencies. The result has been, on the one hand, splendid growth in missionary expansion and theological expressions, but on the other hand, an unfortunate spread of sectarianism and institutionalism. Our background in the Orient has been different; therefore, we may have something to contribute to the understanding of the Body of Christ.

What I shall say is written out of the measure of faith revealed to me through the Word of God by the Holy Spirit. However, it is not merely the product of speculation, but the result of my life-long experience with fellow believers. Far from being purely theory or speculation, this seemingly fantastic and abstract idea *can* be realized in actual experience as it has been for many years in Japan.

The Sin of Divisions Among Christians

There are many foreign missionaries today in Japan who have come from different churches and groups as well as from different countries. The number of denominations and sects seems countless to the average Japanese, for there are over a hundred so-called "Christian" groups. Each have their own unique doctrine or organization by which they distinguish and separate themselves from others. Though some of them are quite tolerant, and willing to cooperate with others, some are very intolerant.

Naturally the Japanese people as a whole are amazed and often disgusted by the divisions and squabblings of those who profess to know the love of God. This cannot be passed off simply as the Japanese ignorance of the church, for many Japanese have found from reading the Bible itself that this condition is contrary to the fundamental teaching of the Word of God.

The *Ekklesia* (translated "Church" in the English edition of the Holy Scriptures) is the Body of Christ.[1] As Head, Christ governs, commands and directs His Body, composed as it is of many members with different gifts or functions. Each member is connected to the Head directly, and thus all members enjoy fellowship with each other through their relationship to Him.

Just as faith in Chirst is a new spiritual life in Him, so the Body is a spiritual organism. This makes the construction of the human body and its members very similar to the essential nature of the Ekklesia of Christ. Indeed, the Body of Christ, though not physical, is not less real and practical than our human bodies. Thus, the Ekklesia has *real* existence, and is *one* Body, and for no reason should be divided. As a human body cannot

1. Ephesians 1:22,23; 4:15,16; 5:23-27, 32; Col. 1:18; 2:19.

live when it is divided into parts, so the Body of Christ cannot live when it is sectionalized. A divided Church is no Church at all in the New Testament sense.

Yet today, to our deep grief, the Church is divided into many hundreds of sects. Though most of them do not openly dare to boast themselves to be the only true Ekklesia, still each of them acts as if it were the only Body of Christ. Having lost sight of the true nature of the Ekklesia, the present day church is divided in spirit and tends to dissipate its strength in fruitless activity and worldly display. *And still more to be feared is the fact that the church does not realize this dangerous condition, and division after division continues without end.*

The serious practical consequences of this condition are more and more obvious. Since the end of the war the innumerable sects of the United States have each been sending missionaries to convert the Japanese to their particular sect — even to the extent of pulling members out of other churches into their own group.

The Japanese are at a loss to know which sect is right in its claim to represent real Christianity. Those who are already Christians are often shaken in faith and hindered in their spiritual growth. Some are led into serious confusion by those missionaries who insist that all Christians who do not hold their particular doctrines are in error.

Even in Corinth where Paul evangelized for a year and a half, contentions broke out among the Christians, who were saying either, "I am in Paul's group," "I am in Apollo's," "I am a Cephian," or "I am just a Christian." Paul said they were carnal and pleaded that they "speak with one voice and not allow themselves to be split up into parties." Rather, Paul said, they ought to agree perfectly in thought and judgment. He gave the same strong admonition in several other cases, e.g., I Cor. 1:10, 16; 15:5-6; Phil. 1:27; 2:2; 4:2, etc.

Far from being of the same mind and judgment, the denominations and sects each have their own banners or trademarks, and boast of their superiority to others, even trying to pull the believers of other churches to themselves. They think that only in this way can they be loyal to the Lord, because they believe that Christianity is represented by their sect alone.

These sects and denominations, with no qualms over "stealing sheep" from other folds, seem more concerned with converting men to their own group than to Christ. Thus Paul's admonitions are so utterly neglected that the Ekklesia of God is now divided into hundreds of sects and denominations and has fallen into fatal disorder.

What is at the heart of this — what is wrong? *All this confusion and disaster is the result of mistaken and false ideas as to the essential nature of the Ekklesia.*

Each church or sect emphasizes its *peculiarities* as the principal elements of Christian faith, and condemns others who cannot agree. As a result, Christianity is heading down a path of endless division, and nobody knows what the end of this path will be.

To clear up present confusion, and to show how Christians may all live as one in Christ, *it is necessary to rediscover the real center of Christianity.* Let us learn what God has made the center of our relationship to Him so that we might make it the center of our faith. Only in this way will the present sin of a divided Christianity be brought to an end.

First, however, it will be helpful to look back and see what has been taken as the center of Christianity in history. In doing so, however, keep in mind that the word "center" is meant to be understood as "the most essential element" of the Christian faith. It might be better to use the word "nucleus" or "essence" instead of "center", but trusting the reader will understand the word "center" as meaning the "essential element", this word will be used hereafter.

CHAPTER TWO

The Center of Christianity Throughout History

1. *The Apostolic Age*

TO THE DISCIPLES Christ was *personally* the center of their faith. He lived and walked with them on earth. His unique personality, His noble character, His heavenly dialogues, His daily life full of love, His miraculous power and His authoritative attitude — all this attracted the hearts of the disciples as a magnet attracts iron.

Believing Him to be the expected Messiah and that the promise of God would be fulfilled through Him, they followed Him everywhere as He preached the Gospel of the Kingdom of God. Their hearts and minds were fully satisfied by being with Jesus. Coming to realize that He was not only a great personality but *God,* they worshipped Him with the same attitude of heart as they had for God. Quite obviously the disciples' faith and experience was centered in *Christ Himself.*

The death of Jesus temporarily threw the disciples into confusion and darkness, but His resurrection restored even stronger conviction to their hearts. Then they began to have intimate fellowship with Him as the risen Lord.

When Jesus ascended to be with the Father, He asked the Father to send the "Paraclete", the Spirit. After this the life of the disciples was united to that of their risen Lord by the indwelling of the Spirit, and they lived a life of *"Koinonia"* — fellowship — with Him and with all fellow believers.

Even in the case of Paul, who had not been with Jesus during His earthly life, this experience of spiritual unity with the risen Lord was most vivid and real, as we can see in his expressions, "To me to live is Christ" and "I am crucified with Christ; nevertheless I live; yet not I, but Christ liveth in me."

The hope of the disciples' Christian lives was the return of Christ, for whom they waited. Their eyes were fixed on the *Lord Himself* as the One who was, and is, and will appear again.

To sum up, the center of the life of faith for the disciples was Jesus Christ Himself *in their spiritual Koinonia (fellowship) with Him.* They were baptized in His name, prayed to Him and worked miracles in His name. They found new life in Him personally, and the purifying hope of His return ruled their lives.

Through the disciples' witness to the risen Christ many were converted to faith in Him. Being baptized, these converts devoted themselves to the teaching of the apostles, fellowship with one another, to the breaking of bread and to prayer. Many wonders and signs were done through the apostles. All who believed were together and had all things in common — they sold their possessions and goods and distributed them to all, as any had need. Day by day, attending the temple together and breaking bread in their house, they partook of food with glad and generous hearts, praising God and having favor with all the people (Acts 2:24-47).

These were the practices of the early Ekklesia, but *none of these practices were the center of their faith.* Their faith was concentrated upon Christ Himself. Their living union with Him was the center of their lives and consequently of the Ekklesia.

The apostles did not think of baptism and the Lord's supper as *sacramental rites* (See John 4:2; I Cor. 1:17; also refer

14

to the Gospels and especially to Luke 22:19, 20 in the RSV). Though they practiced baptism and the Lord's supper as the most valuable expressions of their faith, it cannot be said that they made these acts of fellowship the center of their faith or of the Ekklesia.

Neither did the apostles establish any creeds or doctrines. Even the so-called Pauline theology was not a theology in the present-day meaning of the word. It was only Paul's method of explaining faith. It was his expression of his fellowship with God and Christ, his witness to his having koinonia with the Lord. To understand Paul's explanation of his faith is one thing, but to have koinonia with the Lord is another. *The former should not be taken for the latter and made the center of faith.*

The center of Paul's faith was union with Christ in the Spirit; the same was true of John, as we shall see later, and their theological explanation was only their effort to make the central Person more real to other believers. *They were not theologizing, but testifying!*

In the apostolic age there were some in the group of believers who labored for the Ekklesia, such as the elders and deacons, etc. But these words were only names for those who served the Ekklesia because they were fitted for such ministry. There was not yet anything like an established institution to select them for those labors. Their services were naturally recognized as they demonstrated among the believers their *charismata,* or gifts of the Spirit.

Authority as exercised in the New Testament Ekklesia was not of the legal or institutional kind such as we conceive of today. Like the Lord before them (cf. Mark 11:28-30), leaders among those early believers possessed *only* heavenly, or spiritual, authority.

Their authority was recognized and followed when, and just because, they spoke in the evident power and truth of the Holy Spirit. Even the authority of the apostles was not legal or organizational, being enforced only by the conviction of the Spirit in men's hearts. In just the same way, the service of the bishops (elders) and deacons was completely on a spiritual basis.

Christians in the Apostolic age never thought of making an institutional organization the center of the Ekklesia, nor of substituting human service or earthly authority for the activity and authority of the Spirit in their midst.

15

2. *The Catholic Period*

When the Emperor Constantine made Christianity a national religion, using it as a means for the spiritual unity of the whole empire, the bloody persecutions of the Roman Emperors ceased at last. After that Christianity rapidly spread over the whole territory of the Roman Empire.

In this expansion Christianity developed the organization that made it "the Church", and this institutionalized system became more and more centralized, until at last the Roman bishop became the "Father" of the whole Roman Church.

European civilization is a combination of Greek, Roman and Hebrew cultures. The Greeks are the source of its philosophical and aesthetic elements, the Romans of its legal and political nature, and the Hebrews of the religious phases of European civilization.

Christianity in the Roman Empire could not escape being influenced by Roman culture. Imperial authority, deriving its power now from political and ecclesiastical union, could declare all citizens of the state Christians and members of the institutional Church. As a result, the true nature of the Ekklesia, as the living Body of Christ, was lost within the Church, and the latter became just a legal body regulated by Church law instead of the Spirit. Faith, like the laws of the state, was reduced to a creed, formulated for and remembered by the common members of the Church. Those who did not accept the creed, just as those who did not obey the law, were judged as heretics and punished.

When Christianity was transformed into such a legal institution, it could no more be expected that communion or koinonia with God and with Christ would be the center of the Ekklesia. The center of faith was transferred from spiritual union with Christ, as the Head of the Ekklesia, to the legal government of the Pope, as the earthly representative of the Kingdom of God. The spiritual Ekklesia was replaced by the earthly institutional Church whose center was the Pope. In this Church the fellowship of Christians was no longer the Body of Christ which has life-union with Him, and Christ was no longer the Head who governs His Body, the Ekklesia.

With the establishment of the institutional Church, the worship of God in spirit and truth died out and was replaced

16

by ritual and formal worship. No more could the words of John, that "the anointing (of the Spirit) which you received from Him abides in you, and so you have no need that any one should teach you, as His anointing (i.e. the Spirit) teaches you about everything . . . " (I John 2:27), be applied to the Christians. The members of the Church were now taught only by the ordained officials of the Church.

This was the Roman Church, which insisted that outside of her fellowship there could be no salvation. Without the sanction of the Pope no one could enter the Kingdom of God, because he alone kept the keys of heaven. And without taking part in the prescribed rituals and sacraments conducted by the Church's ordained officials, one was not only unable to be a true member of the Church, but was not even considered a Christian.

Not only did the Church teach this, but these principles became the laws of the Church. Those who refused to obey these regulations were ultimately excommunicated, losing as well their legal rights as citizens and the protection of the state. To stand against the institutional Catholic Church came to be far more serious a matter than to stand against the government of the state.

Under this coercion men's minds were deprived of the right to freely seek truth and real faith. Those who did hunger and thirst after faith and spiritual life had to seek it at the risk of their lives.

Thus the institutional Church, with the Pope as its head, became the center of Christianity. Especially after the system of the Inquisition was established in several countries of Europe, heretics were relentlessly tracked down and cruelly punished by the Church, whose law had the power of the state. The Church had become a purely legal and worldly institution.

It was as the result of this policy of Inquisition that Wycliffe of England, John Huss of Prague, Savanarola of Italy and William Tyndale of England were put to death. History bears witness to the tragic consequences of a system which could render such retribution for translating the Scriptures or opposing the Holy See.

This severe punishment deeply impressed the uneducated masses with the concept that to reject the authorized doctrine of the Church was the worst sin a man could commit, and meant as well that toleration of such heresy was just as bad. So men were led to think that one's Christian duty was to follow the

17

dogma of the Church unquestioningly and to persecute the heretics.

This spirit of intolerance survived even after the Reformation and entered into the Protestant Churches to become the real cause of the lamentable sectarianism of the present.

3. *The Protestant Period*

In the Reformation, Martin Luther and John Calvin established new churches in several parts of Europe separate from the Roman Church. Therefore, the Protestant Christians, the Roman Pope and the Roman institution lost their position as the center of Christianity. What then was to become the center for the new churches that arose out of the reformers' work?

For Martin Luther, as we can see in his commentary on Galatians, the central element of his faith was union with Christ in *Spirit and Life* — that is, koinonia with God. But it was the Holy Scripture that led Luther to this faith, and he fought against the Roman Church, using this Book as his sole weapon.

All the other reformers likewise found in the Bible the whole source of truth. In rejecting the authority of the Roman Church, these men turned to the Scriptures as the authority for their faith and actions. *In the fierce conflict of those early days of the Reformation, it was natural that they should seek the security of some objective standard to meet the seemingly unlimited politico-ecclesiastical power of Rome.* Therefore, the position of the Bible as the God-inspired testimony of the apostles' personal faith in Christ gradually changed and became the source of Protestant "dogma" and the criterion of acceptable faith. *Replacing the Roman Pope, the Bible became the center of Christianity in the Protestant churches.*

Luther's rediscovery of the great Biblical doctrine of "salvation by faith alone" was one of the greatest events of human history. His restoration of the Bible to its rightful place as the basic source of Christianity was real progress. Compared with the faith of the Roman Church, it was a tremendous step in returning to the original New Testament faith.

However, it was now felt necessary in Protestantism, as it had been in Catholicism, to make a clear-cut distinction between orthodox and heretical faith and to exclude heretics from the new, purified church. So there came to be little difference between Protestants and Romanists in their insistence on making a clear, outward distinction between "real Christians" and heretics.

As a result, the Protestants were forced to spend much effort in formulating their own creeds, which produced many excellent statements of scripturai truth, such as the Augsburg Confession of 1530, the Basel Confessions of 1534 and 1536, the Helvetian Confessions of 1536 and 1567, and the Scotch Confession of 1560, as well as the French (1559), Belgian (1562), and Westminster (1642) Confessions.

Though all these confessions were very worthwhile in themselves, still none of them could claim to be the absolute standard of faith. *Faith is life in Jesus Christ and a life can never be confined within certain systems or creeds.* Therefore creeds are not the end or object of faith in themselves, but expressions of our fellowship with Christ, and must not be mistaken for the object or center of our faith. Obviously the fullness of the living Christ cannot be held within the narrow limits of written creeds.

The Bible itself is but the description of this life, that is, a description of God in His relationship to men. Consequently, it contains many seeming contradictions arising from the complex and varied nature of the lives of individuals and their experiences with God. This makes it impossible to sum up the truth of the Bible in any fixed creeds or confessions, because they can never be more than one person's or one group's understanding of the truth.

The failure to understand this limitation of creeds has given rise to unavoidable disturbances in Protestantism, and has become the cause of the division of Christendom into many sects and denominations based on a different interpretation and understanding of certain texts or teachings in the Bible.

The first famous dispute among Protestants broke out between Luther and Zwingli over the meaning of the Lord's Supper. In the year 1529 Philip of Hesse, trying to unify the warring sides of Protestantism, brought about a conference in Marburg, hoping to get Luther and Zwingli to agree on certain principal doctrines.

At the conference they could agree on all doctrines except whether the bread and wine in the Lord's Supper were actually the flesh and blood of Jesus, or only represented them. Because they could not agree on this point they would not shake hands, and at last the conference was dissolved in failure, to the disappointment of all. All European and American Christians know the great harm this disagreement has done to the unity of Christians.

A second episode occurred between Calvin and Servetus. They could not agree on the doctrine of the Trinity, and Calvin finally caused Servetus to be burned on the hill of Champell. The three Reformation heroes in this way became examples of sectarianism and were naturally followed or imitated by their successors, throwing the church into divisions without end. From this beginning many hundreds of sects and denominations have appeared in the world, each thinking itself to be the true church and holding all others to be mistaken. This has continued until now, making it almost impossible for them to be one in Christ.

The points on which the church has been divided will be summarized in the next chapter.

CHAPTER THREE

Points of Division

Theology

THEOLOGICAL CONTROVERSY has raged over many issues, the most basic being now the division between "orthodox" and "liberal" theologies. This has caused great division among Christians, especially when the former falls into dead orthodoxy, rejecting all fresh thought for critical study, and when the latter falls into pure humanism, rejecting the fundamental truths of the Bible.

These two oppose and fight each other, the orthodox condemning the liberals as faithless, and the liberals despising the orthodox as old-fashioned disregarders of science and worshippers of the letters of the Bible (bibliolatry). And there are many other lesser theological distinctions, creating wide conflcts among Christians. So when one takes theology or creed as the center of Christianity, it naturally follows that there must inevitably be a division of Christians into denominations and sects.

Inspiration of the Scriptures

One might think that with the Bible as the center of Christianity, the unity of Christians could be easily realized. Unfortunately this has not proved true, though we *can* consider it fortunate that, as this inability to unify proves, the *letter* of the Bible cannot really replace the living Christ as the center of our faith.

The Bible is the expression of the life and work of God, and since "life" is greater than its manifestation, it cannot be expressed completely in any logical or theological form. Therefore, the Bible itself cannot escape being understood in many different ways. Thus we see how in the wisdom of God it is impossible in practice to make the Scriptures the end or final authority in themselves, for they only express God's authority *to those who live in fellowship with the Spirit.*

On the one hand there are the so-called *fundamentalists* who, accepting the Bible as the "infallible Word of God", believe there is no mistake in the whole Bible, not even in one phrase or manner of wording. To them it is, in the most literal sense, the Word of God from cover to cover, and their faith is utterly dependent on its literal infallibility.

On the other hand there are *liberals* who try to compromise Biblical truth with science. Denying the spiritual in favor of the rational, or adopting the results of higher and lower criticism, they reject the inspiration of the whole Bible.

There are yet others who take the whole Bible to be the Word of God as do the fundamentalists, but in a little different way. They believe that the Spirit acts in the *written* words of the historical records to reveal the *Living* Word. They recognize the Bible as the record of God's revelation of Himself throughout history, climaxing in Christ — an inspired record resulting from the activity of the Spirit in the individuals who wrote it.

Part of the problem in approaching the Bible arises from its very nature, i.e., the way in which God saw fit to give it to us. When the rays of the sun pass through a lens, they are refracted or diffused according to the quality and shape of the lens.

As the Spirit of God worked in history upon those who wrote the Scriptures, the Word of God was naturally recorded in a form "refracted" and "diffused" by the lens of the writers' human nature and historical background.

Just as the study of the quality and shape of a lens is necessary to know the nature of the original rays which passed through it, so to fully understand the will of God through the written record, the circumstances of history in which God revealed Himself and the character of those through whose instrumentality His Word has been transmitted to us must be studied.

Perhaps God allowed these "limitations" of the written record so that *factual* knowledge and *intellectual* understanding of the Bible might not become an end in itself.

At any rate, we should avail ourselves of such studies and knowledge, and seek, in dependence on the work of the Spirit, *to come into personal relationship with Christ, the Truth Himself,* through the Bible. For apart from *both* the written Word and the quickening Spirit there is no real knowledge of the living Word of God.

Interpretation of the Scriptures

Many have put great emphasis on certain texts of the Bible and have built up sects upon those few texts, disregarding the context and the general teaching of the whole Bible. For example, the "Holiness" groups tend to over emphasize the doctrine of sanctification and, selecting some verses which seem to teach it, insist that entire and perfect sanctification it attainable in this life. The "Friends", emphasizing the "inner light" and the fellowship of the Spirit, seem to neglect even such important doctrines as redemption through the blood of Christ.

However, in condemning such extremes, we should remember that these groups may have had sufficient reason for their appearance when, because of dead orthodoxy, many Christians became very loose in their moral lives. Believing that Christ was judged on the cross as their substitute, they neglected the practical results that really believing this truth always produces.

Others, though not falling into loose morality, held the dogmas and creeds of Christianity as a kind of diploma from school or college, or as a ticket into the Kingdom of Heaven. Although having no living fellowship with the Lord, they thought themselves to be the best kind of Christians. They lacked the

23

Spirit acting within them and were orthodox only in their heads and not in their hearts.

Such conditions among the Churches gave rise to those who emphasized holiness and spirituality. *Then, when not accepted by Christians as a whole, they made their doctrine a basis for fellowship within a narrow circle of those who agreed with them.* Thus new sects were born, which in turn tended to disregard other truths and the teaching of the Bible as a whole.

Almost innumerable sects have arisen in this way, and thus Christ's Body is divided into countless sections. Nothing could be clearer than that such doctrinal emphases are a prime cause of sectarianism.

Rituals and Ceremonies

The Baptist Church separated from other churches because of differences of opinion regarding the form of baptism. Another group was divided over whether they should use an organ in their services — because the Bible nowhere tells us to use an organ. Again, a certain sect arose over the supposed necessity of women covering their heads when they pray (I Cor. 11:2-6). Seventh Day Adventists insist on keeping the law concerning clean and unclean foods. There are many such cases, in which very trifling questions about formal rites have given rise to new sects. Then, each sect condemns the others, often calling them heretics.

It is very unfortunate for Japan and other "heathen" lands that many of these sects are sending missionaries to continue these conflicts there.

Conclusion

The Protestant Church is so divided that to realize its unity seems almost hopeless. This has come from mistaking the true center of Christianity and substituting either theology, or dogma, or creeds, or the Bible, or institutions, or rituals, or ceremonies.

Moreover, the divisions were emphasized by the idea, inherited from the Roman Church, that one's own group alone has the orthodox faith and all other groups must be persecuted as being in error. Thus, much vigorous activity is expended in refuting the doctrine of other sects and in trying to pull believers out of them and into one's own sect.

Where is the unity of the Ekklesia? What has happened to the oneness of the Body of Christ? Why do not we Christians recognize the *sinfulness* of this condition and *repent*?

CHAPTER FOUR

The True Center of Christianity

Summary

THE ROMAN CATHOLIC CHURCH, by putting the *Institution,* with the Pope as its head, in the center of Christianity, had ceased to be an expression of the real Ekklesia. This gave rise to Protestantism, which in turn put the Bible in the center, though still largely retaining the institutionalism of the Roman Church. This new center also proved *off*-center and has resulted in splitting Christians into many warring, incomplete sects. Thus Protestants, too, have not realized in practice the true Ekklesia.

Recently, some have recognized the impotency and wrongness of the existing state of the churches and are endeavoring to remedy the situation by reuniting divided denominations. They seek to form an alliance of all churches into one ecumenical Church.

However, this movement, too, is obviously doomed to failure and the very effort to unite the churches seems likely to end only in the formation of yet another great sect or denomination. I say this because the churches involved are *not* re-establishing the true center of Christianity but rather are still caught in the sectarian spirit inherited from Catholicism.

The *Ekklesia* (translated "Church" in the English edition of the Bible) is the Body of Christ. Composed of many members — each connected directly to the Head in spiritual life-union and possessing different gifts and functions — this Body is a *spiritual organism*. Being a single, corporate, spiritual entity— *one* Body — the Ekklesia was never intended to be divided and simply cannot live and function properly in a divided condition. Yet this is the obvious condition prevailing today.

What is at the heart of all this — what is wrong? Where is the true unity of the one Body of Christ? The answer is simple, yet profound. *The confusion and disaster of sectarianism is the result of mistaken and false ideas as to the center, or essential nature of the Ekklesia.*

The True Center

The center of Christianity is neither institution nor organization. Nor is it even the Bible itself, as the reformers made it, for the Ekklesia existed before the formation of the New Testament canon. Christians were in fellowship with God and one another, centering their faith in Christ, long before there was any accepted New Testament.

There is only one center of Christianity, and this center is *spiritual fellowship with God through Christ — life union with God in Christ.* When there is this *koinonia,*[2] there is the Body of Christ, the Ekklesia. Where there is no koinonia with God there is no Ekklesia, because the life-union is lacking. Though there be many excellent clerical personages, many elegant church buildings, many scholarly dogmas and creeds, if there is no koinonia with God and Christ there can be no Ekklesia at all. On the other hand, if there is this koinonia with God and Christ, the Ekklesia exists — we need pay no attention to the differences of creeds, institutions and rituals, but by loving one another can be one in Christ.

2. Koinonia is a transliteration of the Greek word which is translated "fellowship."

Only this union with God in Christ can be the center of Christianity. The Scriptures confirm this, because this fellowship is the theme of the whole Bible from Genesis to Revelation. Indeed, the relation between the Father and the Son in eternity was undoubtedly just this fellowship.

John tells us that "in the beginning was the Word, and the Word was *with* God". This "with", the Greek πρός (and not σύν or μετά which have other emphases) describing the state of being in the presence of a person, is best expressed by "face to face with God" as Williams translates it. Just as the last Adam was thus from the beginning πρός God, so the first Adam was created for the same position of fellowship, and was "face to face" with God in the Garden until the fall.

This is why God created man in His own image. Though the whole creation was "very good" in His sight, still God must have felt very lonely as He found not one among all the creatures with which He was able to have fellowship. All the animals, birds and fish were certainly very beautiful, but they could not come to God and talk and walk with Him in the Garden of Eden. Therefore, He created man in His own image — i.e., able to talk with Him, to meet with Him, pray to Him, and seek after Him. To live with God and to have *fellowship* with Him was the sole object of our being created in the likeness of God.

This communion must ever be the center of the relationship between God and man. Of course, the universe is beautiful in itself, but without the existence of human beings God could never be satisfied. God created man in His likeness, a spiritual being capable of responding to His love and having *koinonia* with Him.

God is Love! If there were no creature who could appreciate His love and respond in love, His creation would fail to reach its fullest consummation.

Even when Adam was driven out of Paradise by God as a result of his fall — the communion broken by sin — this judgment was not to destroy man but to ultimately save him from his fallen state and restore the broken fellowship.

God revealed Himself to Noah and his family to save them out of the Flood. He selected Abraham and his descendants as His chosen people, disciplining them to fit them for fellowship with Himself. How often God appeared to Abraham and talked

27

with him, until he became known as the *"friend* of God". This is nothing else but Koinonia.

God continued to appear to the people whom He sought to *know* — to Isaac, Jacob, Moses and the children of Israel. Leading His people out of Egypt through the wilderness of Sinai, God very often appeared to them as they travelled through the desert. [He had them build the Tabernacle, and later the Tabernacle of David, and finally the Temple, so as to have "just" (righteous) ground for communion with them in the sacrifices.

In fact, one of the most strategic [3] verses in all Scripture is Leviticus 26:11, 12 where the Lord said to Israel, "I will set My tabernacle *among* you, and my soul shall not abhor you. And I will *walk* among you and be *your* God and ye shall be *My* people." This verse is quoted by the apostle Paul in II Corinthians 6:16 as referring ultimately to the Body of Christ and by the apostle John in Revelation 21:3 as being finally, prophetically fulfilled in all the *fullness* of its rich meaning when the "New Jerusalem" comes down from God in heaven, prepared as a bride for her husband. — *The Editor*]

Afterwards God had fellowship, or koinonia, with David, and later with the prophets. In this way God continued to have spiritual union with mankind in the person of these representative men. However, God was not satisfied to have fellowship only with those selected few. He wanted to be united in spiritual fellowship with all the people on earth. Even His choice of Israel as His elect people was only the first preliminary step to salvation for the whole of mankind.

To accomplish this purpose, God ultimately sent His only-begotten Son to earth — "For God so loved the world that He gave His only-begotten Son, that whosoever believes in Him should not perish but have eternal life." Jesus became "the Lamb of God who takes away the sin of the world", paying the penalty of man's rebellion against God, to make it possible to re-establish man's interrupted fellowship with his Creator. Thus, we have "boldness to enter into the *holiest,* by the *blood* of Jesus " (Heb. 10:19).

Fellowship between God and man, interrupted by the sin of the first Adam, was reopened by redemption bought with the blood of the last Adam. Now anyone can have direct koinonia with God and share His very life — anyone can live a life of

3. See Exodus 25:8; I Kings 6:12,13.

28

love and unity with Christ. This is really the center of Christianity, and "faith" is nothing other than the state of having this life union with God. To be justified by faith means that God has *access* to repentant sinners through Christ and is thus able to enjoy this koinonia with them.

If we will practice this living union with Christ, loving each other without any concern about sects and denominations, doctrines or forms, then we shall have the Body of Christ with Him as Head. This is the Ekklesia in its truest and purest sense. Therefore, the Ekklesia is not an institution, not a system, not theology, not the words of the Bible, and not any ritual or ceremony. *The Ekklesia exists where there is this life union with God through Christ.*

CHAPTER FIVE

Understanding Faith and True Unity

F AITH IS THE GIFT OF GOD which produces in us this fellow-ship with God in Christ. *It cannot be created or maintained by human efforts.* With the Spirit of God governing us directly, we love each other and do God's work by obeying Him. *Faith is but another name for fellowship, the koinonia with God.* In this relationship the power of God works through us. No creed or doctrine, no priest or pastor, no institution or ceremony is actually necessary. The *one* thing required is that a man repent and come to Christ for the forgiveness of sins and the newness of life He freely gives.

When the Lord walked on earth, He praised the "great faith" of a centurion and blamed the "little faith" of the disciples. He acknowledged the faith of a sinful woman, a leper, a woman suffering with a flow of blood, and a blind man by saying, "your faith has saved you".

In all such cases no doctrines, institutions or ceremonies were involved. Those who simply relied wholly on the Lord *Himself* were accepted, their sins forgiven, and thus they were saved. The only necessary condition was that they have *faith* in Christ personally — i.e., that they engage in a living contact with Him. Where there was this "faith", there was the beginning of the Ekklesia, because through this koinonia they became one with Christ and He became their Lord.

In a word, Christianity has its center in God Himself, and in the fellowship men have with Him. This fellowship of God through the Spirit with believers is the answer to the question of what faith is, and of what the true Ekklesia is.

When this centrality of God in fellowship with men through Christ is made clear, we at once see that all other elements, such as an institutional Church, the interpretation of the Bible, various doctrines, the morality of believers, or any other problem of different denominations or sects, cannot be the center of Christianity. When this revelation dawns, we know that we should not judge others by any of these standards, for Christ Himself never made these the standard for judging His followers. The center of Christianity is fellowship with God. The Bible itself is not the center. It is only the inspired *description* of this central truth, through which we may come to the center and have fellowship with Him.

Oh, how important our fellowship with God is! This koinonia is the essence of the new *life* we have in Christ. "You pore over the Scriptures for you imagine you will find eternal life *in them*. And it is they that give testimony to *Me*." (John 5:39).

Redemption by the blood of Christ is, of course, the most important fact of Christianity, the basis of all koinonia with God. Everyone knows how Paul emphasized this truth, as also did Augustine, Luther, Calvin and every other great spiritual leader through the years. But "God loved us and sent His Son to be the propitiation for our sins," not just to have us *believe the doctrine* of our sins being forgiven through the blood, but also to let us actually in *practice* "have boldness and confidence of access through our faith in Him" (Eph. 3:12; see also 2:13, 18; Heb. 10:20).

To have access to God is the true purpose of redemption, while the propitiation by the blood of Christ is the *basis* on

31

which we are allowed to come near to God. Therefore, the main purpose of God's sending His Son, as well as the Son's death on the cross, was to let us have this access, this entering into communion with God. We know how God loved us, because He gave His Son to save us (I John 3:16; 4:10). Without the cross of Jesus we would be unable to know the love of God or to be saved from the curse of sin. But only to *know* that He loved us is not enough. We must actually come into His presence and *experience* koinonia with God.

He who acknowledges the doctrine of redemption is not necessarily experiencing the fellowship it allows, but all who have communion with God surely are also trusting Him who forgave our sins through the redemptive death of His Son. This relationship of experienced fellowship with Him is what God really wants of men, for this was the purpose in our creation.

Therefore, merely to understand or confess the doctrine of redemption is only to have found *the passage* through which to come near to God. Those who stop there have not yet come into life-union with Christ and are in danger of dead orthodoxy. How full the churches are of this kind of "faith"!

Because of this we must be careful to avoid making the *doctrine* the center rather than the *life*. There are many Christians who, though for one reason or another may not subscribe to some statement of the *doctrine* of redemption by the blood of Christ, still are standing very close to God and obeying Him from their hearts. Perhaps Albert Schweitzer and Karl Hilty are examples of this. If I had been born in a country where so much dead orthodoxy prevails, I too might have been repelled by such a doctrine of redemption professed without a corresponding change in life and practice.

To confess faith in the resurrection is one thing and to have fellowship with the risen Lord is another; to believe in the doctrine of the second coming is one thing, and to wait for Christ's return is another. For as the *fact* of the resurrection of Christ gives us the *faith* that sees God face to face, so the coming again of Christ gives us the hope that we "shall be caught up together . . . to meet the Lord in the air, and so shall we always be with the Lord." *In all such doctrines, the koinonia with God is the ultimate object expected, and all the various dogmas serve only as tributaries to this main stream.*

Koinonia Versus Institutionalism

When God's people truly see that the center of Christianity is fellowship with God, and that this fellowship is realized through Jesus Christ, then they will see the true causes of the divisions in the churches, and will understand the way to get rid of them. The primary cause of these divisions is the institutionalism and organizationalism of the churches and missions, which instead of helping the life of the believers in them, smothers or drives it out. This gradually produces mere dead institutions instead of the living Ekklesia.

Christians who really have life in Christ cannot exist within such a corpse and usually will finally come out of it. But, sad to say, in most cases those who leave dead institutions simply set out to build another "better" institution or embrace other rituals and ceremonies, thus repeating the same error. Instead of turning to Christ Himself as their center, they again seek to find fellowship and spiritual security on the very same basis that failed.

Even the Bible itself is interpreted and understood in various ways and often becomes the cause of sectarianism. In the same way, dogmas and creeds cannot bring Christian unity, because human minds are not so uniformly created that they can unite in a single dogma or creed. Even our understanding of Christ Himself cannot be the basis of unity, because He is too big to be understood fully by any one person or group. Our limited understandings do not always coincide. One emphasizes this point about Christ, another that, and this again becomes the cause of division.

Only as we take our fellowship with Christ as the center of Christian faith, will all Christians realize their oneness. There are different understandings of Christ. There are varying opinions about the Bible and its teachings. There are various kinds of institutions and ceremonies. But this need not hinder our practicing the unity of the Body of Christ. Is not our fellowship, however varied, with the same Lord? Is not the same Saviour our one Head?

Our fellowship with God in Christ is, as we have seen, the very purpose of God in creating man. In its fullness it is His "eternal purpose" — the Ultimate — and He cannot rest until this is fulfilled, however great the cost may be to Him because of man's sin.

I feel that all Christians are aware that this koinonia is very important, but obviously they have not realized that *it* — not theology, doctrine, creed, institution, ceremony, etc. — is *the* center of Christian faith. When all Christians see this, the change will be amazing. Our practices, of course, will not be the same, because God's commands differ according to the different gifts and callings. But even though each one may differ in carrying out his part of the will of God, since God's object is *one,* all members of the Ekklesia will be united in doing the will of the same God, fulfilling one great purpose. Each individual, by doing his part, will contribute to the work of God in cooperation with others.

God is the great Conductor, and the individual members of the orchestra each play their *varying* parts on *different* instruments; but if all follow the Conductor, the whole composition will be a complete and beautiful *symphony* in perfect harmony.

The ecumenical movement, which has become very popular recently, seems to have arisen from the belief that the division of Christians into many sects and denominations has greatly weakened their power and made it almost impossible to fight against worldly forces, especially Communism. This is true, as far as it goes, but we must remember that the unity of Christians is not a matter of human effort or cooperation. *True unity must come solely from God, and when there is true fellowship with God, it will come naturally of itself.* The power of Christians does not come from human cooperation but from life-union with God. It is the power of God working in men.

Therefore, the One Body cannot be created by human collaboration. It exists through simply removing the barriers and having fellowship with God, a reality prevailing among those who obey Him and love each other. No other merely human method will avail. "Thou shalt love the Lord thy God with all thy heart, and with all thy soul, and with all thy mind . . . Thou shalt love thy neighbor as thyself." This is the law and the prophets — and also the Gospel.

How Can We Tell?

If the center of Christian faith truly *is* fellowship with God and if only those who have this fellowship are Christians

34

and those who lack it are not, regardless of their profession or what institution they are members of, then a serious and difficult problem is naturally raised. Some will say, "How can we tell whether someone is a Christian or not?" Well, in the final analysis, we *can't* really know for sure whether another is a Christian or not. This knowledge belongs solely to God, Who alone can judge a man's heart. No human being can judge another's faith without probability of prejudice and error.

For many centuries the distinction between believers and unbelievers was made by their reception of baptism and the Lord's supper. Yet, who can deny the inadequacy of these standards? Everyone knows that there are many baptized non-Christians and many unbaptized Christians. The confession of creeds and doctrines is also a very inadequate criterion for recognizing Christians, for these confessions can be made without the experience of the new birth.

Actually, we have created a problem that need not exist, for no final decision on a person's faith, or any standard to judge by, is needed for the simple fellowship among Christians that God intended. *Such drawing of man-made boundaries and distinctions is needed only for organizations and institutions.*

However, once we lay aside the *necessity* of objective judgment, we *can* in actual practice, though imperfectly, still tell whether one is a Christian or not. The most important basis for such recognition is, of course, that he confess Christ as his Lord, with the sincerity of a life that demonstrates that Lordship. There will be the reality of loving God and men in practical experience. It is a lamentable fact that there is very little love among thousands who belong to the different churches and sects. This makes us doubt that these are really Christians, for "He that does not love does not know God; for God is Love" (I John 4:8).

Conclusion

To sum up, I believe God is moving to reveal to all Christians what the true center of the Christian faith is, and that the inevitable spiritual unity which will surely result will be one of the major steps toward the fulfillment of God's full purpose — His "eternal purpose". All Christians are *one* Body in Christ — we cannot create this, but only recognize it. However, we *must* recognize it and then fearlessly practice it, disregarding our differences in doctrine, forms and interpretations of the Bible. We must receive one another on the ground of a mutual fellowship with God in living union with Christ in the Spirit. This is the essence of the true Ekklesia, and in such a free fellowship the truth will surely triumph.

On the contrary, if we put our emphasis on other matters, as has usually been the case in the churches since the Reformation, the great mistakes of the Roman and Protestant Churches will only continue. Division upon division will overcome all efforts to perfect the Church, and certainly any attempt to form an ecumenical Church will prove to be in vain.

We simply must come back to this central point, for in no other way can the oneness of the Body of Christ be practiced. I realize that to those who are used to the life of organizational churches, this principle seems very vague and impractical, but if they will put it to the test and really live the life of fellowship with God, practicing fellowship with all Christians upon this basis, they will soon experience the reality of it. Those who have experienced a real measure of this koinonia with God and men, from Apostolic times down to the present, *know* that it is the true and practical center of Christianity, and that here alone is the pathway to the unity of all Christians in the Ekklesia of Christ.

CHAPTER SIX

The Only Pathway to Unity

Summary

IN THE LAST CHAPTER we have endeavored to pinpoint the center of Christianity. We saw that this center is spiritual fellowship (koinonia) with God through Christ. Where there is this *koinonia* there is the Body of Christ, the Ekklesia. Where it is lacking there is no Ekklesia.

We showed that this is clearly confirmed in the Scriptures, this fellowship being the theme of the whole Bible from Genesis to Revelation. In *all* doctrines *koinonia* with God is the ultimate object expected, the doctrines serving only as tributaries to this main stream.

When there is true fellowship with God, true unity will come naturally of itself — *if no man-made barriers are raised*. Therefore, we must receive one another simply on the ground of a mutual fellowship with God in living union with Christ — this is the essence of the true Ekklesia and here alone is the pathway to the unity of all Christians.

The Question of Doctrine

The conclusion that fellowship with Christ is the center of Christianity may give rise to a problem in the mind of some Christians concerning the place of the doctrines of Christianity. For example, take the doctrine of the Cross of Jesus, or salvation by the blood of Christ. Some will say, "Is not the important doctrine of salvation through the Cross being neglected?" or, "Can anyone be saved without redemption by the Blood?" Since this doctrine was the foundation of the Reformation, such questions are natural and justifiable. However, I believe the following points, when plainly realized, will clear away these questions.

First, faith, as the Scripture presents it, is not faith in this or that doctrine, but faith in the *person* of the crucified and risen Christ. And such faith in the Lord Jesus is nothing but this fellowship with Him, by the Spirit who indwells believers. It is not just a conviction but an *established relationship.*

The death of Jesus Christ was the essential *basis* for the forgiveness of sins, because "without the shedding of blood there is no forgiveness of sins" (Heb. 9:22). But the necessity of the death of Christ as ransom for our sins was the concern of God, *"to prove . . . that He Himself is righteous and that He justified him who has faith in Jesus"* (Rom. 3:26).

Throughout history men came to faith in the Saviour-God before He revealed fully how He would accomplish the salvation He offered. Abraham was justified by faith, the Israelites expressed their faith in Jehovah through the ceremony He prescribed, Jesus granted many sinners forgiveness before He died — in all these cases, and many others, the atoning death of Christ was undoubtedly understood in the mind of God as the basis of forgiveness. But those whose sins were forgiven were trusting the Redeemer *Himself,* without knowing some method or theory of redemption.

Faith is fellowship with God in Christ on the basis of blood-bought redemption. It is not knowledge or acceptance of the doctrine.

It is true that only through the teaching of the death of Christ as the great price of our redemption do we come to under-

38

stand the immeasurable depth of God's love for us. The more deeply we realize His love, the more firm will be our conviction that our sins are forgiven, the greater will be our love towards God and the closer our fellowship with Him will become. Knowing God, who is love, we will naturally express Him to others in terms of our experience of redemption through His shed blood.

But there are many whose consciousness of sin is not yet deep enough to appreciate this doctrine of redemption, or whose background makes full understanding of it difficult. Also, there may be some who have been hindered by the dead orthodoxy of those who, professing to believe this doctrine, live a life little different from those who have no faith.

The death of Christ is necessary for the forgiveness of sins, but our understanding of it is not necessarily a condition of salvation.

At the *last* judgment the Judge is not going to be so concerned about the doctrinal confession of those before Him as whether or not they submitted to Christ and obeyed His will. Jesus taught that many who are trusting their correct doctrinal statement or their thoroughly evangelical work will find themselves utterly disowned — *"Not every one that saith unto me, Lord, Lord, shall enter into the kingdom of heaven; but he that doeth the will of my Father which is in heaven. Many will say to me in that day, Lord, Lord, have we not prophesied in thy name? and in thy Name have cast out devils? and in thy name done many wonderful works? And then will I profess unto them, I never knew you; depart from me, ye that work iniquity"* (Matthew 7:21-23).

To the Judge of the living and the dead, theological understanding and doctrinal correctness will have no importance — their *heart obedience* will have revealed whether they really had faith in God. The Lord will judge men solely by what they *are* and *did,* not by what they knew and confessed, except as the confession reveals the heart.

The shed blood of Christ is the means through which every true Christian comes into the living union of fellowship with God. But some may depend upon this means without understanding the meaning of it. They may trust "the One who saves" without comprehending all He does in the work of salvation. Fellowship with God is possible for all who, repenting of their sins and submitting to His Lordship, will come to Him. This fellowship

— koinonia — is the *object* sought, while redemption through the blood of Christ is the *means* of obtaining it.

If doctrine is taken as the center it becomes the cause of divisions, because it makes one prone to judge another's faith by one's own understanding. God gave His Son on the Cross, not to make His redemption — or the understanding of it — a condition of salvation, but that it might be the basis of the salvation, *which is living fellowship with Himself.* The Lord Jesus shed His blood not to raise a barrier to fellowship with God, but to open the way to that fellowship.

Now, if the fundamental doctrine of Redemption should not be put at the center of the Christian faith, how much less all the other theological issues. It is not that these doctrines are unimportant. Quite the contrary. It is a matter of *misuse.* Indeed, if doctrines were not so misused, almost all the causes of division and sectarianism would be eliminated.

The organizational churches, with their doctrines and ceremonies, may be compared to a house and its ornaments. They are useful only if they help the activities of the Spirit in the Ekklesia. But the history of Christianity is full of examples which show that they generally hinder the work of God and tend to choke the life of Christ with outward restrictions, hiding the true Ekklesia and her Head. However, if we put fellowship with God in the center, all these errors and divisions can be avoided.

Israel and Jesus Christ

In the old Testament God continually taught Israel that she should separate herself from the other nations, because she was God's peculiar treasure, chosen by Jehovah and exalted above all nations.[4] Therefore, not only was Israel forbidden to worship other gods and idols, but God made them a separate people by forbidding them to intermarry with other peoples, by directing them to circumcise all males and by various other social and dietary regulations.

This seems to be the strictest kind of sectarianism, and we cannot deny that a misunderstanding of this exclusivism has had much influence on Christianity. It certainly did upon the Jews before us, and Christ was decidedly against this spirit of pride in Israel.

Hear John the Baptist: "Do not presume to say to yourselves

4. See Exodus 19:5,6; Deut. 4:20; 9:29; 14:2; 26:19.

40

'We have Abraham as our father'; for I tell you, God is able from these stones to raise up children to Abraham" (Matt. 3:9). Upon another occasion Jesus said, "I tell you, many will come from the east and west and sit at the table with Abraham, Isaac and Jacob in the Kingdom of heaven, while the sons of the kingdom will be thrown into outer darkness" (Matt. 8:11, 12). Then, in John 10:16, we hear "And I have other sheep that are not of this fold. I must bring them also, and they will hear my voice. So there will be one flock, one shepherd."

It is clear from these and other statements that Christ hated the sectarian spirit and national pride. The separation of Israel from other nations did *not* mean that they should boast themselves above others, but that they should come nearer to God and be taught how they should live before Him without being polluted by the spirit of the surrounding world. The purpose in this was not that they might glory in their national existence and disdain others, but that in their blessings — as an example — they might point all other nations to the one true and living God.

Jesus very often condemned the Pharisees in severe words. But in no case did He blame them because they belonged to the sect of Pharisees, but because of their formalities and legalism. He did not hesitate to have a friendly talk with Nicodemus or to dine and talk with Simon and other Pharisees. He condemned them, not because they belonged to the sect of the Pharisees, but because they prided themselves on having all the truth of God exclusively. It was sectarianism which Jesus hated. The issue was whether they were faithful and sincere, not whether they belonged to the sect of the Pharisees.

Jesus warned His disciples against having this sectarian spirit. In Luke 9:49, 50, John said, "Master, we saw a man casting out demons in your name, and we forbade him, because he does not follow with *us*." But Jesus said to him, "Do not forbid him, for he that is not against you is for you." John wanted the disciples to monopolize the truth among themselves and exclude all those who did not belong to his group. This sectarianism which Jesus condemned, is the spirit which dominated the Roman Church and was inherited by the Protestants.

Jesus insisted that men have faith in Him, love Him and have koinonia with Him: "He who is not with me is against me; and he that does not gather with me scatters . . . I am the way, the truth and the life; no one comes to the Father but by me."

41

In such statements as these, Jesus made it clear that He is the sole and perfect means of salvation, and except through Him there is no salvation (compare Acts 4:12).

But this attitude of Jesus cannot be called a sectarian attitude. He was making the essential distinction between those who were God's and those who were not, not a sectarian distinction among those who were God's. Sectarians are those who would make fellowship with Christ their exclusive privilege. They are not satisfied with belonging to Jesus, they would make Jesus belong to them.

Jesus condemned the Pharisees not because they did not belong to His group, but because of their hypocrisy, untruthfulness and lack of love. He wanted all men to come to Him and have koinonia with Him, but He did not intend that those who did come to Him should have any exclusive group around Him. He chose twelve disciples to preach the Kingdom of God, not to create a sect.

He never flattered people in power, such as Nicodemus and Joseph of Arimathea, enticing them to join His group and help Him. If He had compromised with the Pharisees, He could probably have obtained worldly influence easily. The fact that He never did such things was not simply that He wanted to make his followers honest and sincere, but also because He was communicating *Life,* and building a kingdom *not of this world or according to its principles.*

Jesus had no thought of creating an organization or formal group around Himself, nor did He teach disciples to form any such organized group. Everything was dependent on the Spirit's uniting men to God through their faith. How different Jesus was from those sectarians who, like the Scribes and Pharisees, search sea and land to make a member of their group, only to make him twice as much the child of Hell as themselves (Matt. 23:25).

All that Christ wanted was faith in Himself. He had no interest in any institutional organization with worldly offices and laws. Neither did He give any dogmas or creeds which may be used to distinguish believers from non-believers. When He praised the faith of people, it was not because of their orthodox theology, or the fact that they belonged to some organization, but on account of their simple faith in His person.

Such simple faith in the person of Jesus Christ Himself, apart from *any* doctrinal instruction or theological understanding,

42

is exemplified by the centurion of Capernaum, the woman having an issue of blood, one of the ten lepers of Samaria, the blind beggar of Jericho and the woman of Canaan.[5] Jesus wants us to have this same simple faith in Him. This faith, with its resultant *life in the Spirit,* forms the vital link with God and one in itself constitutes the Body of Christ.

5. Luke 7:9; 8:48; 17:19; Matt. 15:28.

CHAPTER SEVEN

Paul, John and Peter

N O ONE CAN QUESTION the fact that Paul had the deepest
insight into the nature of the Ekklesia. He taught that Christ
is the Head of the Ekklesia and we believers, being joined to
Him as members, are therefore one Body — His Body.[6] When
we believe, we are united to Christ by the Spirit. By faith
alone are we in His Body. And by "faith" Paul meant the same
thing as Jesus Himself — that is, wholehearted love for, and
koinonia with, Christ. He made this clear by citing Abraham as
the great example of faith, though Abraham had no "doctrine"
of redemption.

Without this *living* faith, this life-union with Jesus Christ,
we are not Christians even though we technically believe every
Bible doctrine, are baptized a hundred times, or join a magnificent institution which has world-wide renown.

6. Ephesians 5:23; Col. 1:18; I Cor. 12:1-31.

Then, Paul insisted repeatedly that believers in Christ should be of one mind and live in harmony with one another.[7] He pointed out that just as the various members of the physical body are very different, the gifts and functions of Christians are so different that they may have some difficulty in believing that other members are united to the same Head and compose the same Body.

Thus Paul warns the "ear" not to say to the "eye" that it does not belong to the body, just because it is not like the ear. And likewise he warns the hand not to say to the foot that there is no need of it (I Cor. 12:21). All the members with their different gifts and functions should act in harmony, for each is united to Christ, the Head.

It is true that Paul was very quick to condemn any tampering with the fundamental points of the Gospel. But this was not because of technicalities or sectarian interests, but because the vital question of union with Christ was in danger. If, for example, someone questioned the resurrection of Christ, Paul rose to battle. Why? Because union with a dead man cannot create life. We live in Christ because He lives in His resurrection life.

But in matters of secondary importance, Paul teaches us to be very tolerant with differences in opinion. He gives perfect freedom, often hardly bothering to point out whom he feels is right.

Take for example the questions of whether one should eat only vegetables or everything, or whether or not one day should be esteemed above the other (Rom. 14). He teaches that no one should pass judgment on another's (i.e. God's) servant, but should rather search his *own* heart and life, resolving never to put a stumbling block or hindrance in the way of a brother. Leaving unimportant matters as the personal responsibility of each believer to God, we should live in harmony with one another in the love of Christ, and together, with one voice, glorify the God and Father of our Lord Jesus Christ (Rom. 14:5, 6; I Cor. 1:10).

Paul is said to have been the first theologian of Christianity. This is true in a certain sense, but not in the modern sense of the word. He explained the Gospel quite clearly and systematically out of his experience and revelation, but he never thought of establishing a system of dogma by which to judge whether people

7. Romans 12:16; 15:5,6; Phil. 2:2; 4:2; II Cor. 13:11.

are Christians or not. He only wished to lead sinners to God through Christ, and thus tried to explain the great principles of God's grace in giving us His only-begotten Son.

Paul proclaimed that through Christ's death in our place we can stand before God. Being justified by faith, he affirmed that we have peace with God through Jesus Christ, and thus have *access* by faith into all of His grace. Thus Paul would lead us to the living God and His Son Jesus Christ, *by the Spirit,* and not to lifeless, theological dogmas by our human understanding.

The important thing is coming into union with God through Jesus Christ our Lord, not coming to understand or profess any of Paul's personal expressions of truth.

"The letter kills, but the Spirit gives life." Paul insisted, just as did the Lord Jesus,[8] that men who become slaves of the literal terms of the Bible are killed rather than given life. How much more will they remain lifeless when they become bound within the walls of institution, dogma and regulation.

John

In the case of John the point is even more clear. To him there was no salvation except through faith in Jesus Christ.[9] John makes a clear-cut distinction between those who believe in Jesus Christ and those who do not.

According to John, to believe is to be in ($\dot{\epsilon}\nu$) Him. "I am *in* my Father, and ye *in* Me, and I *in* you" (14:20), "Do you not believe that I am *in* the Father and the Father *in* Me? (14:10). By many such expressions John put great emphasis upon koinonia, or the meeting with God and Christ.

John did not give us any system of doctrine about theological questions, much less any kind of dogmas. His writings are so different from Paul's systematic and logical way of teaching that one is often at a loss to find out the main point of discussion or how he is going to develop his argument. He seems always to be endeavoring simply to describe the "Life *of* God, and *in* God" in its living status — to catch the Life as it is working. Life in Christ is a continual experience of Christ and not a theory or a dogma.

While I was compiling the *Greek-Japanese Concordance,* I found a very interesting fact about the Johannine writings. The

8. II Corinthians 3:6; John 6:63.
9. John 1:12-18; 3:16-18; 8:12; 10:9; 14:6; I John 5:5.

noun "faith" πίστις was to be found only four times in Revelation and once in I John. But John uses the *verb* "believe" πιστεύω abundantly. In his Gospel he uses it about three times as often as all the Synoptic Gospels put together.

Also, John never uses the word "pray" or "prayer" in his writings (except when the word ἐρωτάω, which really means "asking", is translated "pray" in the A.V.). I do not think this was an accident. John saw "faith", not as a formal concept to be formulated into some theological expression or dogma, but always *a living and moving experience, more fitly expressed with a verb.*

John was interested only in Christ, the *object* of faith, not in "faith" as a thing in itself. For John, the life of a Christian was a life with God in Christ. Prayer is talking to God and can never be done apart from koinonia with Him. Since koinonia is fellowship with God, the life of koinonia is itself a life of prayer. When John did not use the word "pray" or "prayer", he did not mean that there be no such thing in the Christian life. Quite the contrary. The Christian life itself should be nothing but prayer, or a praying life.

In just the same way, though John never uses the word "Ekklesia", except in Revelation, he clearly understood the true meaning. The believer shares the life of Christ as a living part of Christ Himself just as a branch shares the life of the vine. This means, just as Paul taught, that Christ is the Head and the Ekklesia is His Body.

In I John 1:3, John points out that the life of fellowship with Christ and the Father is a life of fellowship with one another. Only in the one who loves others does God abide (I John 4:12, 16). He states firmly that only those who have the Son have life and that he who has this life lives in a relationship of love with other Christians (I John 3:14).

Thus, it is indisputable that John, although he understood the true Ekklesia, never conceived of an institutional church or a union of Christians on any other basis than *life.*

Peter

Peter does not say a great deal about the Ekklesia. However, a close reading of his epistles reveals the same principles we have seen in Paul and John's writings. He exhorts believers to be holy in their lives — both as Christians and as fellow-citizens of a heavenly nation — to be of one mind, having compassion and humility and to love one another earnestly from the heart (I Pet. 1:16, 22; 3:8). This was for Peter the basic principle of the unity of the Ekklesia — the *spiritual* house made of *living* stones of which Christ himself was the cornerstone (I Pet. 2:4-7). He had no idea of establishing an organized church upon Christ as its foundation.

The foregoing has been but a brief outline of the concept of the Ekklesia as taught in the Holy Scriptures. If you study further, you will find that the principles hold throughout. There is no idea of institution, of legal authority and offices, nor of definite sacramentalism, at least as of central importance.

CHAPTER EIGHT

The Essential Nature of the Ekklesia

THE EKKLESIA IS THE BODY OF CHRIST, and its Head is Christ Himself. This Body is a *spiritual organism*. The Head and the members are *actually* connected spiritually, and because of this connection there is true fellowship with Christ, each member loving Him in heart, mind and spirit.

This fellowship is faith in its purest sense. To have faith is to rely upon Christ, *the Person,* with the whole heart. It is not the understanding of the mind, not theological opinion, not creed, nor organization, nor ritual. It is the *koinonia,* or communion, of the whole personality with God and Christ which is itself the continuation of the real attitude of dependence on the Saviour which we call faith.

Where there is this fellowship there is the Ekklesia, because there is the real Body of Christ. Where there is not this fellowship, there is no Ekklesia, though there may be baptism, the Lord's Supper, institutions, church offices, good works or anything else. Human activities and devices cannot make or form the Ekklesia, and it does not exist outside of this fellowship of Christians with Christ.

Distinguishing Christians

Because it is a *spiritual* relationship, fellowship with God and Christ cannot be seen with human eyes. However, the reality of this relationship reveals itself in the life of the believer by his confession of faith in Jesus Christ, by his Christian love towards others and by his obedience to God as demonstrated in his conduct. Also, when one is truly a Christian, he is sensitive to this faith-fellowship in fellow Christians and this results in the growth of Christian friendship.

If we could know conclusively whether one is a Christian or not simply by whether or not he is baptized it would be very convenient. But unfortunately, as is so obvious here in Japan, the churches are impatient to make baptized members, often trying to induce, sometimes even to compel, seekers of the Gospel to be baptized. The consequence of this premature baptism is that many of them fall away afterwards, not even attending the church meetings, much less evidencing real faith. No one would say that these people are Christians because they were once baptized.

Then, is holding the right doctrine the real mark of a Christian? Yes, actually. However, there are some who later doubt the teachings they once accepted, perhaps because it was more of a mental acceptance than a heart faith. Others make a confession of faith from emotional feeling, while some are not completely sincere when they make confession. Consequently, this also, cannot be a certain means of distinguishing true Christians.

Likewise, the acceptance of the creeds should not be taken as a proof of one's being a real Christian, for such acceptance does not necessarily imply full understanding and experience of these statements. There is a big difference between the acceptance of doctrines or creeds and fellowship with God. The former is a question of reason and knowledge, while the latter is a question of the Spirit's giving *life*.

It is obvious that no human means exists for distinguishing clearly between believers and unbelievers in border-line cases. The methods of distinction upon which the churches and the

50

Christian groups are based can only result — as experience continually proves — in including some who do not really know Christ and excluding some who have His life. In this sense, the existing churches cannot be considered to be the same as the Ekklesia, or true Body of Christ. Serious confusion has resulted when churches have assumed attitudes or prerogatives proper only to the Body. We must always clearly distinguish between the churches of men and the Ekklesia of Christ — the Body in which He *lives*.

At this point perhaps you are thinking, "If we cannot perfectly distinguish between Christians and non-Christians, how are we able to have fellowship with Christians?" To those who are used to the practice of churches this is a normal question, for it is confusing for them to think of Christian fellowship outside the outward distinction propagated by their church group.

Such anxiety is unnecessary, however, for God who purposed and created this fellowship has provided a very real and practical foundation for its realization. *Our problem lies in the fact that we have come to doubt that the spiritual relationship God has given us to Himself and one another is sufficient as the basis of true and full fellowship.* This doubt exists only because such free and simple fellowship has been so long hindered and hidden by the bonds of institutionalism. We must let the life-giving power of the Spirit set us free from this false ecclesiasticism if we are ever to realize true Christian fellowship.

The new life which we are given at our new birth, though spiritual, is a *real* life and will express itself in practical living. The Christian's daily life reveals his faith in both words and deeds. For example, he witnesses to his faith in the Lord Jesus without being ashamed. Those who are having fellowship with the Lord will not find it difficult to locate their fellow believers. All who are "looking to Jesus, the source and perfecter of our faith", will readily recognize each other as having the same characteristic of life. *This might be called an instinct of the new life.* The stronger the faith, the keener this sense; for those who are having the most vital fellowship with Christ in this new life can most easily identify those who have the same life.

Another important point to grasp is that in the light of the true Ekklesia *it is not necessary to circumscribe the Body of Christ.*

Churches find it necessary to do this in order to carry out

their organizational activities and functions, but Christ said, "Where two or three are gathered in My name, there am I in the midst of them." Even when there is no church building or official leadership, still Christ will be in the midst of those who are gathered in His name. This is the essence of the real Ekklesia, even though there may be no "church", as such.

When those confessing Christ are really living a life of fellowship with the Lord, they will realize in practice the true fellowship of the Ekklesia with all other Christians as a matter of course. That is, *if* all other elements, such as creeds, rituals, institutions and understanding of the Bible are secondary. *Their fellowship with each other is then entirely the result of their fellowship with Christ,* thus this *koinonia* with Him is truly their center. When united on this simple New Testament basis, Christians will be tolerant of differences of opinion and practice in secondary matters. They will love each other with the love of Christ, and in this love we see the hope of that oneness of all Christians for which we yearn.

"Everyone who acknowledges Me before men, I will also acknowledge before My Father who is in heaven" (Matt. 10:32).

"Man believes with his heart and so is justified; and he confesses with his lips and so is saved" (Rom. 10:10).

"Whosoever confesses that Jesus is the Son of God, God abides in him and he in God" (I John 4:15).

Thus one's confession of faith, unless belied by his life, is proof that he has living koinonia with God and has become a member of the Body of Christ, the Ekklesia. But "if anyone says, I love God, and hates his brother, he is a liar" (I John 4:20); so we can generally tell by the conduct and the attitude of a person's daily life whether his confession is sincere or not.

Moreover, those who really have fellowship with Christ cannot but propagate the Gospel. Among non-believers they will witness to the truth, not only by word of mouth but by doing good works and by not fearing persecution from the enemies of God. Those to whom spiritual gifts are given, especially gifts of teaching or preaching, will be using this ability. In this way God will cause the Ekklesia to grow from faith to faith.

Church (Ekklesia) Life

This koinonia — living in fellowship with God and Christ,

having access to God and meeting Him in love and faith — is the real Ekklesia. In such *experience* of life, Christians will meet together, worship God together, help one another and do various good works in cooperation. As is natural in human society so in the Ekklesia, there will be division of labor according to the varieties of gifts (I Cor. 12:27-28). Everything will be controlled by the Head, Christ, and each member will do his own part in obedience to the will of the Head.

No human institutions, rituals or ceremonies are necessary to realize this. The Ekklesia cannot be formed by human knowledge and human activities. Indeed, it was of these products that the tower of Babel was built. The institutional church may have some outward likeness to the Ekklesia, but spiritual fellowship with God and Christ is more stifled than helped by the formalities of the church.

The *legal* unity of human organization, which is so often governed by men appointed by human methods is substituted for *spiritual* unity. By its very nature — being an institution — the organized church is prone to become fleshly ($\sigma\alpha\rho\kappa\iota\kappa\acute{o}\varsigma$) rather than spiritual $\pi\nu\epsilon\upsilon\mu\alpha\tau\iota\kappa\acute{o}\varsigma$. Also the existing sectarianism is itself a proof of fleshly-mindedness. "For while there is jealousy and strife among you, are you not *of the flesh* and behaving like *ordinary men?*" (I Cor. 3:3). The Ekklesia, on the other hand, is a product of the Spirit. It is, therefore, absolutely necessary that *spiritual* means be employed in its government and edification.

If we do not give the rightful preeminence to koinonia with God through Christ as the center of Christian faith we cannot but fail, for there are only two courses before us. Aside from secular atheism and the materialistic concept, if we do not find satisfaction through communion with God — for which we were created — then, invariably, we will try to find reality and satisfaction in the "Churchianity" of institution, forms and doctrines. *Lacking spiritual "life", we turn to "religion" — the lifeless corpse.*

CHAPTER NINE

What About Sects and Denominations?

I F THEN IT IS TRUE that the Ekklesia exists wherever there is fellowship with God in Christ — and the consequent fellowship among believers — what about the existing churches? How should we react to all the creeds, dogmas, doctrines, interpretations of the Bible, ceremonies, sacraments and legal systems?

Variety Essential

In the first place, we should not deny or seek to avoid the fact of variety in doctrinal and practical matters. Man is a creation of God and God does not create like a factory, by mass production. Every person is individually created by God as an independent being and is, therefore, more or less different from all others. We err if we expect to find mechanical similarity among men, even among the children of God. The Ekklesia is *one* Body consisting of many independent, though inter-dependent, personalities. Even biological science tells us that the more life is developed the more complex its construction.

Some believers have deep theological insights, others passionate evangelistic tendencies, some this gift and some that gift; also there are differences in race and language, in degree of education and in social customs. Each have our own special duty to fulfill as a result of the differences of God-given gifts and circumstances. These differences, however, ought not become the cause of divisions. *Why do we think that division is always the only alternative to uniformity or sameness?* The innumerable varieties of the human mind show the intended manifold character of the Body of Christ. Each member should not only *retain* his distinctiveness, but should also develop his special gifts in order to be able to serve the *whole* Ekklesia and make his necessary contribution to the fullness of Christ in His Body.

In this sense, the different emphases of many denominations and sects are *not* bad in themselves. These very differences would profit the whole Body if each group would only be humble enough to recognize the value of the others, instead of making their differences the basis of exclusivism and separation.

It is not only unnecessary but actually harmful to endeavor to nullify the differences and make a mediocrity out of them — and still worse to try to unify them by political or ecclesiastical power. Instead of condemning or excluding those whose knowledge or understanding is different from our own, we should love them, thanking God for what He has given us in them. Although it is quite *natural* (fleshly) that these differences be the cause of divisions, Christians must not yield to this worldliness. It is pride that despises others who are different. If we will *respect* different tendencies, in love for each other, this variety of the local groups of Christians will contribute to the Body of Christ, rather than hurt it.

It is just such differences which have caused sects and denominations. The existence of these varied characteristics is, in itself, not to be condemned; but instead of appreciating how greatly we need the contribution which those who are different can make to our faith, we have made our own differences a rallying point — *substituting for Christ our special expression of Christianity as the center of faith and fellowship.* As a result, what God meant to be a blessing to the life of the Body has become a curse, dividing Christians into little groups, separating them from each other. Everywhere we see believers putting fellow believers out of their fellowship and rejecting, condemning and despising those in whom Christ lives. How awful in God's eyes is the sin of disobeying God's command to love *all* Christians, not just in spite of, but *because of* their differences.

Can we so lightly ignore the Apostle Paul's words, "I therefore beg you to lead a life worthy of the calling to which you have been called, with all lowliness and meekness, with patience, forbearing one another in love, eager to maintain the unity of the Spirit in the bond of peace." He goes on to show that the basis of this attitude is in the seven-fold unity that makes us *one* in Christ. "There is *one* Body and *one* Spirit, just as you were called to the *one* hope that belongs to your call, *one* Lord, *one* faith, *one* baptism, *one* God and Father of us all, who is above all, and through all and in all" (Eph. 4:1-6).

In the human body the eyes, mouth, nose, ears, hands, feet and many other physical organs each work according to the purpose for which they were created, never intruding into the sphere of the others' work nor belittling others' functions. Each fulfills its "calling" according to the command of the head. The foot does not say, "Because I am not the head, I don't belong to the body"; nor does the ear say, "Because I am not the eye, I don't belong to the body." The eye should not despise the ear because it cannot see the beauty of nature; likewise, the ear should not condemn the eye because it cannot hear beautiful music (read I Cor. 12).

Saying this, however, does not mean that the Christian can believe anything he likes, and that any kind of faith equally will be Christian faith. No, there is one essential which we can never dispense with — the living fellowship with God and Christ. This is the center of Christian faith, without which — or opposing which — no one really can be called a Christian. Christ *Himself* is the object of our faith and we believe in Him *as a Person,* not just in facts about Him. Whatever ideas or concepts we hold must find their source and focus in the One who, as the object of our faith, is that Rock from which flows the water of *life.* Without this *life* (indwelling Spirit) we are none of His.

Unity in Diversity

A most helpful teaching on this theme is found in the 14th and 15th chapters of Romans. There Paul uses the example of differing opinions about food and days among the believers in Rome to teach that Christians should not despise or judge one another. *Note that he does not advise them to find a happy medium between the contending opinions or to average the two extremes into a compromise.* On the contrary, he admonished that "every one be fully convinced in his own mind". He declares that God is able to make *both* stand, since both are serving the Lord in obedience to their individual conviction of His will (cf. verse 4). The weak in faith should not pass judgment on the strong, and the strong should not look down on the weak.

In this connection, it is also totally unscriptural to define the will of God by a majority vote. God's will cannot be defined by the wishes of the majority; therefore, each of us must find personally what is the will of God for himself. Each must do what he believes to be the will of God for his own life, and let all others meet their responsibility to do the same. The will of God may differ for each of us, but that does not matter. By giving different commands to many, and putting them together according to His plan, God shall accomplish ultimately His complete will. *Individual* responsibility is necessary for doing the will of God, because God's will is compound and complex, differing according to each person concerned.

On the other hand, Paul tells us that we should live in *harmony,* "being in full accord and of *one mind*" (Phil. 2:2). He says we should "be united in the *same mind* and the *same judgment*" (I Cor. 1:10), and "live in such harmony with one another in accord with Christ Jesus, that together we may *with one voice* glorify God".

The question, then, is how those who are "fully convinced in their own minds" of *different* convictions are able to be like-minded and with *one mouth and one mind* glorify God. Is it not obvious that this can only be realized if the one essential center, out from which our whole Christian experience flows, is the love and oneness of spiritual fellowship with God in Christ?

This is unity in diversity and diversity in unity. The true Ekklesia has neither uniformity nor conflicting differences, neither individualism nor collectivism. It is *one* living Body, with *diverse* members.

This is a strong admonition against the sectarian spirit of the churches. The God-given differences, which should contribute to the fullness of the one Body, have become cause of division instead of unity. Each sect and denomination has its own institution and creeds. When there is a difference among the members of a church, some of them separate themselves from their fellow-Christians and form their own institution and creed. Such an institution and creed clearly distinguishes that group from all the others and thus becomes the cause of division.

Only Basis for Division

This raises the question as to whether or not anyone should ever be excluded from Christian fellowship. The answer is quite evidently yes, but we must be careful to notice the Scriptural circumstances of such exclusion. According to Paul, such cases arise when there is someone among the brethren who commits gross sin. Paul instructed the believers "to stop associating with any so-called brother if he is leading the life of a fornicator, a greedy grasper, an idolater, a slanderer, a drunkard or a robber — even to stop eating with such a person."

Such "believers", if they prove incorrigible, will have to be considered as *un*believers (Matt. 18:15-17). However, such separation is not among Christians, but is rather the expulsion of those who cannot be accepted as Christians in spite of what they profess. If we allow such sinful people to mingle with the members of the Body of Christ, the Ekklesia, it is as if we allow infectious germs or a malignant growth to remain in our physical body — the whole body will be corrupted.

There is a fundamental difference between immorality or Christ-denying doctrine and the variations in doctrine or practice found among individual Christians who basically have Christ as the center of their faith. While the former will corrupt and destroy the Body of Christ, the latter will make up the completeness of it. Therefore, the one ought to be rejected and driven out, while the other must be accepted and treated as God-given contributions to the fellowship.

This, of course, does not mean that *all* doctrinal differences ought to be accepted. When Paul reminded the believers of the essence of "the good news which I proclaimed to you, which you accepted, on which you are now standing, through which you are saved — unless your faith at first was spurious" (I Cor. 15: 1-2), he must have intended to emphasize the importance of what he had preached. His message was that "Christ died for our sins in accordance with the Scriptures, that He was buried,

58

that He was raised on the third day in accordance with the Scriptures, and that He appeared to Cephas, then to the twelve . . . " (I Cor. 15:3-5).

At that time there were some "Christians" who insisted that there is no resurrection of the dead. This presented a very serious problem for Paul, because the center of faith was fellowship with a *living* Christ, He "who died for us and rose again from among the dead". Therefore, this difference was not a question of theological opinion, but a denial of the essential basis of the Christian faith — i.e., the fellowship in the Spirit with the risen Jesus. If Jesus did not rise again, this fellowship with Him was only sheer fantasy, lacking reality, and "then our preaching is in vain, and your faith is in vain" (I Cor. 15:14). Paul could not be silent about this.

But even in such a case as this, Paul was not thinking of excommunicating those people who did not believe in the resurrection, for he had no institution or organization from which they could be excluded. Being convinced that they had no living fellowship with God, he sought to *persuade* them about the fact of the resurrection. By this attitude he demonstrated what a Christian should do when confronted with those who disagree on important, central facts and teachings of the Gospel. Rather than driving out at once those people who did not understand the resurrection, he wished to help them understand the true Gospel and come into living fellowship with the risen Christ.

The Issue Defined

In conclusion, we return again to our reaction to the existing sectarian chuches. It is true that these usually have their origin in those variations and differences which must be recognized and appreciated for their needed contribution to the life and fellowship of the whole Body. However, we are forced to conclude that the organizations and institutions men have built on these differences have only hindered and interrupted the life of the true Ekklesia. History has proven this to be true again and again. Even at their best, they do not add anything to the reality and practicality of the koinonia with God in Christ, which the Spirit produces in the Body of Christ. Believers, who are outside the sects and denominations, will find no need of them in having full and complete fellowship with God and men in the Ekklesia. As to those who are within, though they need

59

not give up their institutional organization, they certainly must face squarely the issue of obedience to God in the practical out-working of the unlimited fellowship He has meant them to have as members of the whole Body of Christ.

CHAPTER TEN

Various Issues Clarified

D IVISION, CONFUSION AND LIMITATION is written over present-day Christendom. The sectarian spirit has paralyzed the glorious experience of believers being one great Body in Christ. Yet in the midst of all this — even in the darkest moments since Christ — there have continued to be those who enjoy a living fellowship with God and all others who fellowship with Him.

The grace of God and the powerful presence of the Spirit have created and maintained in the world, even within the entanglements of religious institutionalism, a "peculiar people" which the New Testament calls the Ekklesia. This simple, living fellowship, or koinonia, was *replaced* by (not *produced* by, as many would think) the "churches", which have attempted to express spiritual life in institutional, creedal and ceremonial form.

A careful study of this Ekklesia reveals certain basic truths, which we have sought to clarify in the preceding chapters but which it might be helpful to summarize here:

The center of Christianity is fellowship with God through Jesus Christ. This relation to God is simply the state of having personal faith in the Lord Jesus, that is, of being in living union with Christ in the new, spiritual life which the indwelling Spirit gives the true believer.

All who are truly in living relationship to God are joined to all others who have this relationship in this same kind of fellowship. This koinonia with other believers is called "the Ekklesia" and is, like the koinonia with God called "salvation", based upon the common possession of the life-giving Spirit.

The Ekklesia, as the Body of Christ, is a living organism, composed of all who are in fellowship with God. Institutions, organizations, creeds, doctrines and ceremonies are not essential to this fellowship. None of these serve to determine who is truly a member of the Body and who is not.

Each member is designed by God for a necessary contribution to the whole Body. The gifts of the one Spirit, as He works through individuals, makes them more or less different from one another, though all have the same fellowship with Christ.

The inherent unity of the Body of Christ must not be impaired or hindered by anything. The organization, doctrines and ceremonies, which some may use to express their life in Christ, *should never restrict the fellowship, or be made its center.* Differences in understanding and practice are normal, and even healthy, and not a reason for division and pride among Christians.

Now, in reaching the conclusion that fellowship with God in Christ is the true center of Christianity, we find that many problems are solved.

For example, Christians will come *naturally* to live as one Ekklesia, in fellowship with God, where this can never be as long as we retain our present conception of the church.

Also, this reveals why many so-called orthodox Christians, though they confess the best doctrines, act very unChristian, while others who doctrinally are rather far from orthodoxy often are more worthy to be called Christians in their way of life.

The former, though doctrinally correct, have missed the essence of Christianity, and their behavior reveals it. The latter, though perhaps confused somewhat in their minds, have pressed through to *life* and the fruit of that koinonia with God is evident to all.

Another stone of stumbling to many is the seeming difference between the teaching of Paul and that of Christ in the Gospels. Jesus stressed doing, while Paul taught faith. However, when it becomes clear that the center and final essence of both their teaching is life-union between God and man, we then see that the difference is a matter of *emphasis* and any argument about "Christ *or* Paul" is absurd.

Again, formerly it was believed that a militant defence of the orthodox doctrines was one sacred duty of Christians, thus placing the emphasis upon the head and knowledge rather than the heart and its reaction to the dealings of God's Spirit. Now, we realize this to be misplaced zeal. It is union and fellowship with God — the new *life* in Christ — that must be defended and proclaimed, and then the needed doctrine will follow naturally *from its true and proper source.*

History bears witness to what I am saying. If institution, organization, creeds, rituals, etc. become the center of Christian faith, then either the life of the Christians ceases to be the life of Christ, as in Catholicism, or the Church is broken into many fragments as in Protestantism.

When we see this simple truth the "golden rule" (Matt. 22: 37-39) is seen in its right light and becomes vital in the life of the Ekklesia. Though no one has ever doubted that this law of love is the noblest teaching of Christianity, there have been many in Protestantism who, in their insistence that man is saved by faith alone, have failed to recognize this as the basic expression of koinonia with God.

Sad to say, the ecumenical church movement is moving on the same mistaken road as earlier organizations. It is good that they seek unity among Christians, but they would do better to emphasize toleration and love among all the sects and denominations, and to make the institutional and organizational boundaries of these groups as loose as possible, instead of trying to create one super-organization — the ecumenical church. This, at least, would put their movement on the right road and be a healthy start toward the full realization of the Body.

Another point of perplexity has been the importance of the writings of John in expressing the fundamental truth of the Ekklesia. As John's teachings were practical and experimental rather than logical, they did not find their rightful position in the theology of the Church. Instead, the epistles of Paul, because they were more theoretical and logical, were overemphasized by the institutional organization, to become the principal source of theological disputes and divisions.

The New Testament is only an extension and fulfilment of the Old in presenting koinonia with God as the central truth. And Paul and John are one with Christ in teaching the same truth, only from different angles.

CHAPTER ELEVEN

Romanism as the Origin of Sectarianism

T HE ROMAN CHURCH BLAMES the Protestants for division, saying, this is our due reward for the sin of severing ourselves from the real Church. This accusation seems justifiable at first, for while there has been little division in the Roman Church, Protestantism has suffered from endless division into sects and denominations. However, the guilt actually lies with the accusers.

The Roman Church is the most complete and best-organized totalitarian regime in the sphere of religion — the *logical conclusion of the assumption that the Ekklesia is institutional in character.* For more than a thousand years it held the Christianity of Europe in its grip, and in cooperation with worldly powers, was able to have complete sway over all Europe.

This unified control was exercised through consolidating dogmas, hierarchical organizations, and enforcing discipline upon its members. Note the three sides to this sectarian triangle: *con-*

solidation of dogmas, hierarchical organization and the enforcement of discipline.

To achieve *conformity* the Church used the severe punishment of excommunication, which meant that the condemned lost his privileges of citizenship and legal protection from the state, as well as membership in the Church and hope of salvation. This was extended by the system of Inquisition, in which those who were against the dogmas, teachings or laws and institutions of the Roman Church were given over to the civil government for execution as heretics.

This combination of ecclesiastical and political powers, with the oppression and persecutions practiced by them, had a tremendous influence on European nations which subsequent history has not yet effaced. Men were so afraid of being branded heretics that few dared to even think of criticizing the doctrines of the Church. Hardly anyone had the courage to study these doctrines to determine whether they were really true. In this way the Catholic teachings, organizations and hierarchical authority came to be thought inherently holy and above criticism. The people of Europe, with very few exceptions, submitted to this ecclesiastical domination and thus came to be the faithful defenders of the Roman Church.

Persecution of the opposition is an inevitable evil policy of all totalitarian systems. This is true in the East as well as in the West. During the two and one-half centuries of the Tokugawa regime in Japan (1623-1867) that government had absolute control over the entire country. When the Portuguese empire expanded and its Roman missionaries promised to become the enemy of the totalitarian Tokugawa government, Christianity was prohibited. All Christians were very severely persecuted and Christianity suffered almost total annihilation.

Now, in order to have their people approve this policy, the Japanese authorities spread abroad horrible, unfounded rumors that the Christian religion was so abominable in its practices and teachings that it would destroy the nation. Thus the people in general, without knowing what Christianity was, believed it to be the most pernicious religion in the world and therefore justified the persecution of it by the government. This mental attitude has persisted even until the present day, so that most Japanese try to keep away from Christianity and abhor from their heart the conversion of one of their family. You see, the Japanese were educated to hate Christianity and to feel a patriotic responsibility to annihilate this dangerous faith.

This is an excellent illustration of the principle that operated among the European peoples under the domination of the Roman Church throughout the Middle Ages. When men are under the same social and religious conditions, over a period of time they come to accept the existing order as the unchangeable truth. Since the Roman Church order taught the people to hate heretics and defend the integrity of the Church's teachings, the people believed it their *duty* to do so and, therefore, had no toleration for heretics.

The reformers themselves were educated in this same atmosphere, so they also thought it necessary to defend the true faith intolerant of any heretics. The only difference was that for the Protestants, Catholics were heretics and true faith was now the evangelical faith. Also the Protestants, for the most part, lacked the power to persecute the Roman Church, so they only fought against it. Because they could not exterminate Catholicism, they had to be satisfied with merely separating themselves from the bondage of its authority.

However, the reformers did not stop with separation from Rome; for having broken free from its bondage, *they made their own institutional church*. Then, almost immediately there appeared differences of opinion among them, and having learned well the lesson of sectarianism from the mother of that spirit, they now believed themselves to be the defenders of the true faith. Their only recourse to difference of opinion was separation, so there started an endless principle of division. This has been especially widespread where there is much individual liberty, as in England and the United States of America. In such countries, where religious freedom makes the development of differences easy, people who are very earnest in defending and propagating what they think to be the only truth have no qualms about separating themselves from others, though they cannot persecute them.

In Germany and Scandinavia where political powers supported the Reformation movements, things did not go so far, but even there the spirit of excluding heretics persists. Naturally, ways of expressing an attitude vary with each generation. Because separation from other believers with whom we do not fully agree no longer involves actual physical persecution, it is thought to be right — and, therefore, is all the more serious.

Since the great reformation leaders themselves took this intolerant spirit, even against the other Protestants, their followers could not be expected to do otherwise. The persecution of the Puritans and other independents by the Anglican Church, the resistance against the free church movement among the Lutherans, the intolerance of the New England Puritans, and many other divisions in Europe and America have come from this spirit of sectarianism still living among Protestants.[10]

Thus the Body of Christ has been divided into innumerable sections. And even more lamentable is the spirit of pride in boasting about such separation as a defence of the purity of faith, while actually disregarding the central essence of true Christianity. Oh, beloved brothers and sisters in Christ, this sectarian spirit, which sees heresy in even small differences of theology, practice and institution, should never have been brought over from the Roman Church. It has no place in the fellowship of true Christians. Such a spirit is inevitable in such an institutional system as Romanism since it is the only way to achieve unity in an institution; but the Spirit of God living in the Ekklesia makes sectarianism not only unnecessary but a *sin*.

May God grant each of us grace to simply rise above *man's* church and dare to realize the freedom and reality of the simple Church Jesus of Nazareth founded.

10. For a thorough historical study of this principle through the centuries since Christ, we recommend the dynamic new book, *The Torch of the Testimony* by John Kennedy (distributed by Voice Christian Publications).

CHAPTER TWELVE

Is This Unity Possible ?

T HE ECUMENICAL CHURCH movement has become an important element in the Christian community of the present generation, but insofar as it tries to create unity through creeds, institutions and organizations, there is little hope of anything but disappointment and failure. In fact, as I mentioned earlier, it is all too probable that this movement may create another new sect with new dogmas and institutions.

It is very difficult to unify the creeds and institutions of many hundreds of denominations or churches. Indeed, it is almost impossible, because many of them have very special kinds of creeds and interpretations of the Bible, of which they are so proud that it would be suicide for them to abandon or change them.

If an attempt is made to find the largest common factor of the creeds of the many hundreds of sects, the result will be

69

simply, "We believe in one God", and all other important creeds will have to be ignored. If on the contrary they try to find out the least common multiple of the creeds, such a creed would have to contain several contradictory ideas, which will mean nothing as a creed.

Even "fellowship with Christ and God" could not work as the creed of such a conglomerate institution as many are seeking to realize. This fellowship or koinonia has no unmistakable outward signs that would fit such a situation. Koinonia is a *fact,* not to be included in doctrines or creeds or institutions or rituals, *but to be experienced.*

As we take this koinonia as the center of Christian faith, refusing to have any creeds, institutions or the like as the essential and central element, our unity consists of *love.* We are united in that love which we have towards those whom we sense to be fellow-Christians by their confession of Christ and their daily life of faith and love.

This may seem very vague and uncertain to those who want some outward signs as the proof of one's being a Christian; but all who have in any real degree experienced it know that in the daily life of believers the love of God will make the unity very real and practical. Was it not true with that little group who believed in Jesus right after Pentecost (Acts 2:43, 44)? On this ground we can have one Ekklesia in love. There may be many differences in opinions, but no enmity.

At present there are all the sects and denominations standing side by side. Each thinks that it is the only true Church, or at least the most correct expression of it. Each believes it is their duty to convert others to their faith. They put large "labels" on themselves, showing the special points of their faith. They advertise their own brand of Christianity to get as many converts as possible. They put special weight and importance on their trade-marks or special creeds, making them as conspicuous as possible. They condemn the goods of other "dealers" as of inferior quality and admonish people not to buy them.

Thus, on the Christian market the different brands are competing with each other in their selling campaign, just like businesses in the world. Sometimes they may have joint campaigns against paganism, but finally they are not satisfied until each boasts of its own superiority over the others. In this way the

70

churches can never have true unity, however much they may say they want it.

On the other hand, unity is quite possible if Christians simply live in fellowship with God and with Christ, and at the same time with one another, accepting the differences in the understanding of the doctrines and other smaller distinctions as reasonable variations due to individual, personal distinctions. As we realize that this variety will, in many cases, make the life of the Body of Christ more complete and abundant, we can even respect differences and in love mutually help to make the Body of Christ grow.

In taking this attitude we shall never be puffed up in our faith and thus shall be able to keep the admonition of Paul to the saints in Philippi: "If there is any consolation in Christ, if any comfort of love, if any fellowship of the saints, if any affection and sympathy, fulfill my joy by being of the same mind, having the same love, being in full accord and of one mind. Do nothing through strife and vainglory, but in humility of mind esteem others better than yourselves. Let each of you not look on his own things, but every man also on the things of others" (Phil. 2:1-3).

The glorious unity of the Ekklesia can be realized only in this attitude of *love* — forbearing and tolerating each other, respecting the special gifts of others, and thus perfecting the Body of Christ. We must abandon the attitude that "orthodoxy is *my*-doxy and heterodoxy is *thy*-doxy" and unite in loving fellowship with God and Christ.

Then, as Paul says, "Speaking the truth in love, we may grow up into Him in all things, which is the Head, even Christ: from whom the *whole* Body joined and knit together *by every joint* with which it is supplied, according to the *working of every part in its measure,* causes the increase of the Body for the building up of itself in *love*" —(Eph. 4:15-16. See also Col. 2:19).

This is the real unity of the Ekklesia, the Body of Christ. Since it is an *organism,* there is no human method of producing it. Life as an organism has its source in life and not in any organization. *As long as Christians think of themselves in the form of an institution, there can be no unity in Christ.* The churches in their present state can never be united, because their very existence is based on the principle of division in the attempt to limit fellowship and visibly distinguish faith.

71

The Ekklesia does not need uniting, because its very existence is based on the fact of an already existing unity. That unity is the glorious unity of our all being *one Body in Christ,* which Body, by its very *life,* is in constant communion (koinonia) with the living Christ. Oh, beloved fellow believers, if we see this simple and wonderful truth, let us dare to let go of everything else and *experience* it. God grant it to be so!